# *The Echoes Return Slow*

*Also by R. S. Thomas*

Song at the Year's Turning
Poetry for Supper
Tares
The Bread of Truth
Pietà
Not That He Brought Flowers
H'm
Young and Old
Selected Poems 1946–68
What is a Welshman?
Laboratories of the Spirit
The Way of It
Frequencies
Between Here and Now
Later Poems: a Selection 1972–1982
Experimenting with an Amen

# The Echoes Return Slow

## R. S. Thomas

MACMILLAN
LONDON

First published 1988 by
MACMILLAN LONDON LIMITED
4 Little Essex Street London W C 2 R 3 L F
and Basingstoke

Associated companies in Auckland, Delhi, Dublin, Gaborone,
Hamburg, Harare, Hong Kong, Johannesburg, Kuala Lumpur,
Lagos, Manzini, Melbourne, Mexico City, Nairobi, New York,
Singapore and Tokyo

*British Library Cataloguing in Publication Data*
Thomas, R. S.
    The echoes return slow.
    I. Title
    821'.914    P R6070.H65/

ISBN 0–333–46806–6

Typeset by Wyvern Typesetting Ltd, Bristol
Printed in Hong Kong

—◇—

Pain's climate. The weather unstable. Blood rather than rain fell. The woman was opened and sewed up, relieved of the trash that had accumulated nine months in the man's absence. Time would have its work cut out in smoothing the birth-marks in the flesh. The marks in the spirit would not heal. The dream would recur, groping his way up to the light, coming to the crack too narrow to squeeze through.

I have no name:
time's changeling.
Put your hand
in my side and disbelieve

in my godhead.
Her face rises
over me and sets;
I am shone on

through tears. Charity
spares what should be
lopped off, before
it is too late.

———◇———

A scrubbed door-step, clean enough to be defiled by the day's droppings, circulars, newspapers. A threshold of war, unbeknown to the young couple, the child-planners, choosing the capital of a fake nation to be their home; the father travelling in 'oils and grease' in between rougher surfaces of the ocean.

———◇———

The scales fell from my eyes,
and I saw faces. I screamed
at the ineffectuality
of love to protect me.

A dislocation of mind:
love photographed
the imbecility of
my expression and framed it.

As though war were cricket matches and jam tarts. The figure in white flannels occasionally had gold braid. The syrens wailed from the berthed steamers. I lay in a bunk while they feasted, turning and turning the glossed pages. The cockroaches should have been a reminder. The shadows from which they crawled were as dark as those where the submarines lurked.

And beyond those silk
curtains the weed
sways that is Salome
dancing before a salt

throne, asking only,
when the dance is complete,
the head of the twice-
baptised on the sand's platter.

The war to end all wars! After 'the hostilities were over', the return to cross-channel. So many hours at sea, so many more on shore. The salt waters were spat into from Welsh mouths. Dreams were laid at the roots of a boy's curls. The sea-horses were ridden by dark riders. Watching steamers was more exciting than watching trains, though sometimes the harbour was a forest of masts, where ships of sail sought shelter from the storm.

There was this sea,
              and the children
sat by it and said
nothing. A ship passed,
              and they thought of it,
each to himself, of how it was fine
there or irksome
                        or of little account.
The sun shone and the sailors
              were faces at the air's
window. They were going
home: one to his wife's lips,
or his wife's tongue;
                        one to remember
this was not what he had seen
              from the ship's bridge.
                        The whirling propeller
beat out the time, but nobody
danced. And three people looked
over a slow surface at three people
looking at them from a far shore.

9

Gathering mushrooms by the light of the moon. The sounds from the town were the clinking of money in an empty vessel. The clouds towered. Their shape was prophetic, but there were no prophets. Through long hours, inhaling the dust that was not injurious, he was prepared with a minimum of effort on the part of himself to 'satisfy the examiners'.

With cash in the one,
no harm in the other,
they persuaded all
but the child, who knew

with a child's roguery
whichever he touched
of the hands held out
would always be empty.

———◇———

No muscle. All legs. His cleverness was in running away. He came to, miles from home, among others who had arrived also, but for their own reasons, wiser than his. Young men and women with one foot on the ladder, confident because of their head for heights that life was a thing meant to be climbed. He studied, he danced. He was half prepared for everything but life.

In time's telescope
all women became
one woman, burning
like a star in her own

sky. And all men became
one man, and I
was that man, eager
to woo, and I lost her.

—◇—

The building towered above the town, a fortress not of power but of learning. He tried to believe they were the same thing. He tasted freedom in a parent's absence. He tried infecting the whiteness of the moon-lighted stream with the seriousness of his shadow. In long trousers, with no money in his pockets, he pretended to forget the black gown he wore was a kind of mourning for his dewy boyhood.

—◇—

He rationed his intake
of knowledge. On fine days
with the mountains leaning
over him to whisper

there were other picnics
beside the musty sandwiches
in the library. Foolish
youth, doing only

enough work to enable
him to answer set
questions, failing the less
gentlemanly examination

of death. 'Eileen died
yesterday' . . . the bruised
sunlight, the rift in time
he was powerless to repair.

So he was ordained to conduct death, its shabby orchestra of sniffs and tears; the Church renowned for its pianissimo in brash scores. At the funeral of the collier's child, when his eye should have been on the book, he saw, with raised eyes, the wild drake mallard winging skyward to disappear into a neutral sky.

Our little boy he paint a tree.
We keep it safe for him.
There is no soil

too good for this tree, but he dead
we plant it rather in our hearts.
There is no fruit on it but his.

———◇———

The first peace had but sown dragon's teeth, not the Welsh dragon's. All night the freight trains thundered over the viaduct on their way south. The English coast was in danger. The tall headlines in the papers marched grimly into an uncertain future. The innocent could not believe the robin could whistle in deaf ears. Its breast should have been his warning.

In the country house
doorway the wind that ruffled
the woman's skirt came
from no normal direction.

Skies were red where no
sun had ever risen
or set. He learned fear,
the instinctive fear

of the animal that finds
the foliage about its den
disarranged and comes to know
it can never go there again.

Others were brave. Whether volunteering or conscripted, they went forth to the war, as their fellows had done hundreds of years. 'Would not have missed it for worlds.' Yes, action has its compensations. What does one do when one does not believe in action, or in certain kinds of action? Are the brave lacking in imagination? Are the imaginative not brave, or do they find it more difficult to be brave? What does a man do with his silence, his aloneness, but suffer the sapping of unanswerable questions?

Entered for life, failing
to qualify; understudied
for his persona, became identical
with his twin. Confronted
as the other, knew credit
was his for the triumph
of an imposture. Slipped easily
into the role for which
his double was cast, bowing
as low as he to appropriate
the applause. When volunteers
were called for to play
death's part, stood modestly
in the wings, preferring rather
to be prompter than prompted.

——◇——

Rumours of bestiality. The old, scarifying
stories about each other kept by nations in the
cupboard for the next time. An unwillingness by
some to recognise war as the lesser of two evils
exposed at the tribunals to the satisfaction of
whom? Casualty of the quarrel with strong men,
bandaging himself with Yeats' sentence about the
quarrel within, he limped on through an absence of
sympathy. His poetry was bitter.

From meditation on a flower
you think more flowers will be born
of your mind? Eichmann meditated
on music and played on his

victims' limbs the symphony
of perdition. I have watched
the tendrils of flowers with less strength
than a child's fingers opening

the hard rock. You know what flowers
do best on. I think how the bodies
of the centuries have been rendered down
that this one should emerge, innocent of
    compassion.

—◇—

What had been blue shadows on a longed-for
horizon, traced on an inherited background, were
shown in time to contain this valley, this village
and a church built with stones from the river,
where the rectory stood, plangent as a mahogany
piano. The stream was a bright tuning-fork in the
moonlight. The hay-fields ran with a dark current.
The young man was sent unprepared to expose his
ignorance of life in a leafless pulpit.

I was vicar of large things
in a small parish. Small-minded
I will not say; there were depths
in some of them I shrank back
from, wells that the word 'God'
fell into and died away,
and for all I know is still
falling. Who goes for water
to such must prepare for a long
wait. Their eyes looked at me
and were the remains of flowers
on an old grave. I was there,
I felt, to blow on ashes
that were too long cold. Often,
when I thought they were about
to unbar to me, the draught
out of their empty places
came whistling, so that I wrapped
myself in the heavier clothing
of my calling, speaking of light and love
in the thickening shadows of their kitchens.

―◇―

The voices of temptation to disregard Words-worth's advice to the poet questioned his shining alone in such murkiness of the spirit. How much is a bird's song worth? What market value has fresh air? Memories of the learning he had neglected drove him to efforts to catch up. Imaginary congregations in enlightened parishes hovered above the heads of his peasants. But the fields were too strong. The woods were holier than a cathedral.

Around you the bunched soil;
above you the empty sky —
it is sufficient for you that every pore
should take a little of their meaning.

Myself I need the tall woods,
so church-like, for through their stained
windows and beneath the sound
of the spirit's breathing I concede a world.

＿◇＿

But life in the remotest backwater is prompter of a hundred and one questions. As to be alive is to be vulnerable to pain, so it is to be conscious that peace is transitory. Reason is open to the blandishments of the machine. The horse was removed from the horse-fly as reservoir of blood. The tractor invaded the age-old quietness of the land. As the war proceeded, technology directed its infiltration. The farmer changed his allegiance from Ceres to Mars, from subsistence to profit. The priest again questioned his vocation.

I saw the land and it was not
waste-land, but one tilled and computed
for harvest. And a voice, that was no
saviour's voice, had said to the breakers:
Be still. And there was a false calm
there, with the scarecrow standing
in it like an old totem of the soil
fallen on bad days, left to the
times' irreverence and the rain's phlegm.

And I waited there at the gateway
on the uncertain boundary between
road and field, not sure of where
I belonged: whether on the conveyor-belt
of the traffic, or out in the soil
as though at the foot of another
cross with a different saviour
on it, and one never to come
down, because of his human rags.

How far can one trust autumn thoughts? Against the deciduousness of man there stand art, music, poetry. The Church was the great patron of such. Why should a country church not hear something of the overtones of a cathedral? As an antidote to Ancient and Modern, why not Byrd and Marcello? But was winter the best time?

It was winter. The church shone.
The musicians played on
through the snow; their strings sang
sharper than robins in the lighted interior.

From outside the white
face of the land stared in
with all the hunger of nature
in it for what it could not digest.

A priest's work is not all stewardship, pastoralia. In a rural parish the time for that is the evening, when the farmer nods over the fire. In the morning, the mind fresh, there is the study, that puzzle to the farm mind. The books stood in rows, sentinels at the entrance to truth's castle. He did not take it by storm. He was as often repulsed as he pretended to have gained ground. And yet . . .

And this one says to me:
                    You are an occasion
merely; an event synchronous
with other events,
                         not caused by them.
I switch my attention.
There are voices superannuating
            the Bible. I must learn,
they say, to believe in a presence
            without existence.
                              Is it
the Orient infiltrating
            our science, or science bringing
a myth up to date?
                    In a dissolving
            world what certainties
for the self, whose identity
            is its performance?
                         You have no address,
says life, and your destination
is where you began.
                    But love answers it
in its turn: I am old now and have died
many times, but my rebirth is surer
            than the truth embalming itself
in the second law of your Thermo-Dynamics.

———◇———

Time passed. The war ended. There were
celebrations of victory in a struggle they had not
fought. The only casualties had been the old
wisdom, the old skills of the land. And the people
with commodities to sell were the richer. With the
lifting of a cloud on the horizon, the desire of a
woman re-asserted itself for someone to cherish
beside the beloved. Close as they were, her solil-
oquies were too soft. He re-interpreted them with
a poet's licence.

I know fair days:
his lips to mine,
his child growing in me.
Selah! But fair as well

that time we lay
all night, side by side,
the moon virginal,
his sword naked between.

The hours were long, waiting for the child to speak, waiting for that breaking of silence which is the unique sacrament of man. With unconscious wisdom he spoke to it, sang to it, wheeled it up and down the valley to snatches of Welsh rhymes, English doggerel. The child lay in its pram, eloquent in a language only the birds understood.

And this little finger says:
'I was not there.' And this one:

'I was in somebody else's
pie.' And the third, pointing

in no particular direction, accuses:
'It was you.' And we look up

away from ourselves, encountering
the sky, that sometimes we take,

so inscrutable its expression, for God's
face, venerable with cloud,

staring back at us and enquiring
with bland ingenuousness: 'Who? Me?'

'The Child is father of the Man ' said Words-
worth. 'The words are wild,' said Hopkins. Despite
the atmosphere of the nursery, that half-light
before the fire, cradling the child, telling it stories,
wishing it God's blessing in its small cot, dark
thoughts come to the priest in the church porch at
night, with the owl calling, or later at his bed-side.

—◇—

Night after night I point my hands
at the sky, a launching pad
for my prayers to take off for their orbiting
in immense space. What listener
is this, who is always awake
and says nothing? His breathing
is the rising and falling of oceans on remote
stars. The forbidden tree flourishes
in his garden and he waters it
with his own blood. Is there a leakage
from his mind into the minds
of our inventors? From earliest
childhood their fingers have been busy
tinkering with the lock on the door
into a dark room. The combination
is yielding. What will come forth
to wreak its vengeance on us
for the disturbance? I lift my face
to a face, its features dissolving
in the radiation out of a black hole.

---◇---

The child growing imperceptibly into a boy; the strange plant that has taken root in one's private garden. The apple of the mother's eye. The grudging acknowledgment by the male, so different from the female, that this also is a twig on a branch of the tree of man. The father's share in the promise of fruit and his resentment at canker.

He was sometimes a bad boy,
slovenly, vain, dishonest.
Yet I remember his lips
how they were soft and

wet, when I kissed him
good-night; and a shadow
moving away from the bed's
head, that might have been God's.

A priest has two gardens, one feeding the body and one the mind. He is trained more for the one than the other. He discovers a quicker calendar in his own garden. What he plants comes up soon. In the church-yard garden everything waits. Is the meaning, then, in the waiting? The stones face expectantly towards the east.

At the grave's head
the book open, a plea
for the tongue not to remain
stone on eternity's

threshold. The weather
has worn the words
smooth, but moss brightens
the spread pages, wings

of a dove daily
returning from its journey
over the dark waters
with green in its bill.

—◇—

Memento mori! But he was young for death. Was the sea calling him on or back? It was a false voice in the trees. Bad days were when three herring-gulls cried above the valley; or when a shepherd in the high moors said: You can almost smell the sea to-day. From different motives he assumed a cure, where that same sound was no longer a trick of the wind, but real waves on the bar a few miles to the west. He was reminded all too soon that journeying is not necessarily in the right direction.

—◇—

The wrong prayers for the right
reason? The flesh craves
what the intelligence
renounces. Concede

the Amens. With the end
nowhere, the travelling
all, how better to get
there than on one's knees?

—◇—

There are sins rural and sins social. Does a god discriminate? Education is the refinement of evil. The priest is required to make his way along glass-sown walls. It is easier to divide a parish than to unite it, except on Sundays. The smell of the farm-yard was replaced by the smell of the decayed conscience.

And this one with his starched lip,
his medals, his meanness;
his ability to live cheap off dear things.

And his china-eyed children
with their crêpe-de-Chine hair,
product of a chill nursery,

borrowing nastiness from
each other, growing harder and thinner
on the days' diet of yawns and smirks.

His wife and his friends' wives,
reputations congealing about their mouths
cutlery after the prandial remarks.

What shall I say more?
Why should I rummage among
the envy, the malice,

the patched-up charm in humanity's
wardrobe, draughty habiliment
this for the candid heart that would keep itself
    warm?

The problems are never only external, although everybody endeavours to make them so. To study is to think. To think is to raise questions that are unanswerable. 'About that of which we cannot speak, we must needs be silent.' He evaded Wittgenstein, if not the publisher, by committing his silence to paper.

An obsession with nothing
distinguished him from his co-
thinkers. From dreaming about
it, he woke up to its immense
presence, to a consciousness
of when he was not, to
the equal certainty
of his being extinguished. It was
a mental property, inherited
on his coming of age; the
recessive thought that,
when progress is about
to be guaranteed, returns one
to the void.
    What parentage
has truth? There was an absence
that was prior to it. God,
too, that defenceless orphan
of a purpose? He looked over
the world's edge and nausea
engulfed him. He was not one
who could balance himself
on the brittle tight-rope
between dark and dark, nor
use his wings in the vacuum
of his disbelief. There was a hope
he was outside of, with no-one
to ask him in, where he stood
with such stars over him
as were like love only
in the velocity of their recession.

To an islander what is the sea for but to go to? After the waves' thunder and the winter's rains, the sky opens its blue eye and the sands formicate. The holiday season brings the multitude from England to the Welsh coast. Are they in search of the bread that perishes? They come; they sit down in ranks, although the grass there is marram. And at summer end the eye is flecked momentarily with migrating birds.

—◇—

Five thousand
of us; the clouds rising
in a blue oven, the sea
with its gold scales. No

miracle. The sand is the crumbs
of an old loaf. The mind
has more than twelve baskets
to fill. The picnic is over.

When the English colonise a parish, a vicar's is chaplain's work . . . officers' mess, receptions. He lied about his ability to play Bridge, but social occasions required at least his inability to circulate. To whom must a priest confess scurrilous thoughts? Blake said that a fool should never enter into heaven, be he never so holy. He did not quote that in his sermons.

—◇—

'How good of you to come!'
                    (Yawning inwardly.)
So beautiful!
          (The bitch!)
Why cannot one avoid
these sparrings?
                    Outside Jupiter
is shining. Everything
is what it is. 'But our beginnings
never know our endings.'
                    Eliot said that.
My superiority surprises
me, but I circulate
where I am, keeping the temperature
boiling.
          'Handsomest of men!'
Can eyes be believed over the rim
of Madeira?
               I signal from behind
smoke leaves, hiding my cleft
foot; tuning my pipe
to the music of tobacco.
The door into the garden
is of plain glass; too many eyes
would attend us.
               I move
to a new partner, polishing
my knuckles, dazzled by the medals
he has left off. Once
in the sand it had been his club
against my fish-net. Here we exchange
insults civilly.
               I slide an eye
at my watch. Early yet.
How take leave of my hostess
without appearing to disengage?

———◇———

Faces looked up at the pulpit, knowing the vicar as a player of games. Young faces waiting to be amused. Is God funny? Is he a sportsman? What tricks has he beside lightning up his capacious sleeves? And the boys' parents, educating their sons to make money as a gentleman should, inclined to concede that religion could be a capital concern.

A congregation at prayer
telling Him what he is like:
You who can do anything
you please; who steer our courses
through secondary causation, bringing
us home safe to a good
meal and a loving family
round a contented hearth; you
who can replenish the empty
belly of Asia, so anachronising
our Lent; who, producer yourself,
can appreciate the brilliance
of our performance, continue this care
since never on to the platform
of a star stepped a species
more deserving.
                    Does God listen
to them, crouched as he is
over the interminable problem
of how not to cheat, when the hell-born
spirit appears to be winning?

———◇———

There come times when it is necessary to evacuate the ear of the echoes of cloying Amens. He walked on the shore again to cauterise his nostrils with raw salt, to refresh his ears with the white waves tumbling thunder. Others walked there, too; women figures like those of Troy, gathered to watch the tilting of innumerable riders. Like Graves before him, his eye fastened upon one woman.

—◇—

'Agh!' I thought, 'one of James' women,
it seems, separating herself
from the crowd, having her splendid
moments, staring with all her sex's
wistfulness at the robust
sea, ready at any infringement
of the privacy of her performance
to retaliate as only a woman

can.' Approaching her, I saw
she was not that kind at all,
but driven to the extremity
of herself by the forces which
she resisted; a woman formed for
desire, but repudiating even the velleities of it.

The highway ran through the parish. The main line ran through the parish. Yet there were green turnings, unecclesiastical aisles up which he could walk to the celebration of the marriage of mind and nature. Otters swam in the dykes. Wild geese and wild swans came to winter in the rush-growing meadows. He hummed an air from Tchaikovsky quietly to himself. Yet on still days the air was as clerestories in which the overtones of gossiping voices would not fade.

A will of iron, perforated
by indecision. A charity
that, beginning at home,
ended in domestication.
An uxorious valour
so fond of discretion as
to defer to it
as his better half. Voyeur
of truth because of an ability
to lie sideways. One
of life's conjurors, standing
upside down on his conscience,
producing out of a hat rabbits
where his brains should have been.
A man with principles so
high as to be out of sight
of his fellows, wrestling
in the small hours with the angel
over the irresponsibility
for life's evil to which
both of them laid claim.

Salving his conscience in the face of the Gospel's commandment to judge not with the necessity for the writer of poetry to be his own critic. The creative mind judges, weighs and selects, as well as discarding, in the act of composing. Yet honesty is without mercy, punishing the practitioner along with the patient.

—◇—

What I ask of humans
is more than human
so without idolatry
I can follow. While he,

who is called God, now
scorches with sparks of
blood, now glaciates me
in the draught out of his tomb.

The cure of souls! Congregations tend to get older. There is no cure for old age. And the old tend to be sick. When one should be leading them on to peer into the future, one is drawn back by them into the past. The visitation of the sick! A ministry more credible because more noticeable than the cure of souls.

They keep me sober,
the old ladies
stiff in their beds,
mostly with pale eyes
wintering me.
Some are like blonde dolls
their joints twisted;
life in its brief play
was a bit rough.
Some fumble
with thick tongue for words,
and are deaf;
shouting their faint names
I listen;
they are far off,
the echoes return slow.

But without them,
without the subdued light
their smiles kindle,
I would have gone wild,
drinking earth's huge draughts
of joy and woe.

On the threshold of middle age, not too old for the young. He listened, trying to sympathise with their assault upon silence. They could converse amid cacophony, but not endure nature's silence. Up in the hills they looked at one another appalled and turned on the transistors. He addressed them, but was not heard. His voice was wind out of the past through a patched gate. Sitting with them in milk-bars, watching them drink their poison, he was unable to prevent his mythopoeic instinct from tangling with the juke-box.

It was a drenched face
too noble for the table
it was being entertained
at by a curled youth
with only a guitar's repertory
to his name. He talked, it
listened vacantly to him
as the sky will to the things we say.

But this was a face from the legends
of the species, that had seen
love burn and lovers go forth
to the wars, and waited without
hope, but without bitterness, for
someone worthy of it to return.

—◇—

For some there is no future but the one that is safeguarded by a return to the past. After the initial, forced move eastward, he had been moving gradually back. Away to the north-west, visible as an unpeopled shadow over the water, was a headland from which he could look back over forty miles of sea to his boyhood some forty years distant. He removed there, unsped, but unlamented. Was his poetry wiser than his action?

———◇———

Are you coming with us?
On the road to Emmaus
you made as if you would go
on, but stayed when they asked you.

On a different road it is we
are for going on, but 'Stay'
you say, contemporary with a future
never to be overtaken.

A bough of land between sea and sky with the clouds for apple-blossom, white by day, pink towards evening. This is where he had crawled out, far as he could go, repeating the pilgrimages of the saints. Had he like John Synge come 'towards nightfall upon a race passionate and simple like his heart'? Simple certainly. There is an intellectual snobbery. The simplicity of the Sacrament absolved him from the complexities of the Word.

The breaking of the wave
outside echoed the breaking
of the bread in his hands.

The crying of sea-gulls
was the cry from the Cross:
Lama Sabachthani. He lifted

the chalice, that crystal in
which love questioning is love
blinded with excess of light.

One headland looks at another headland. What one sees must depend on where one stands, when one stands. There was sun where he stood. But on the pre-Cambrian rocks there was also his shadow, the locker without a key, where all men's questions are stored.

Years are miles to be
travelled in memory
only. The children have vanished.
Here is what they saw

over the water: a beetling
headland under a smooth
sky with myself absent.
How shallow the minds

they played by! Not like mine
now, this dark pool I
lean over on that same
headland, knowing it wrinkled

by time's wind, putting my hand
down, groping with bleeding
fingers for truths too
frightening to be brought up.

Both window and mirror. Was he unique in using it as a window of an asylum, as glass to look through into a watery jungle, where life preyed on itself, ferocious yet hushed as the face of the believer, ambushed in a mirror. So much easier for the retired mind to lull itself to sleep among the reflections.

—◇—

Spun seas, clearer than my thoughts
                    that I lacerated
with my hooks . . . I would have opened
them on soft hinges
                           and leaning far out
called the fish to my lips
to share their breath with me
                    before gliding back
                                on silk wings
painlessly to the branched fathoms.


                    It was not
to be. There were sombrer ways
            of lubricating the sluices
through which life pours, and with no-one
to answer to but this dissenting
member of your economy you took them.

---◇---

White skulls, oily with dew in the late moonlight. Rising before dawn, he peered into a field as into a cemetery of white grave-stones. His feet rustling in the wet grass, he moved from one to another like an angel, not to raise but to gather them in a meshed basket. Forty years later he did so again, the sun on his hand. Nature was still bountiful, but man was erecting, beautiful and poisonous, the mushroom-shaped cloud.

—◇—

'Not done yet,' mutters
the old man, fitting a bent
poem to his broken bow.

'Of all the Middle Ages . . .'
said Byron. So I refine
my weapons: beams, gases;

composer of the first
radio-active verses. Ah,
me! When I was a child,

innocent plagiarist,
there was dew on the early-morning
mushroom, as there is not now.

In the order of things children bid fare-well to their parents. Unable to hear his father bid him fare-well in his stentorian voice. He was buried in a grave in a town by the sea. Seven years he waited for his wife, dragging the bones' anchor in the colourless fathoms. And then it was her turn, too feeble to speak. The woman, who all her life had complained, came face to face with a precise ill.

She came to us with her appeal
to die, and we made her live
on, not out of our affection
for her, but from a dislike
of death. Her face said she looked
in that stone face; its vocabulary
made her tongue dry. Her breath
was that of one keeping afloat
over bottomless fathoms; and we waved
to her from the solider shores
of our own flesh. The ambulance came
to rescue us from the issues
of her body; she was delivered
from the incompetence of
our conscience into the hospital's
cleanlier care. Yet I took her hand
there and made a tight-rope
of our fingers for the mis-shapen
feelings to keep their balance upon.

Minerva's bird, Athene noctua; too small for wisdom, yet unlike its tawnier cousin active by day, too, its cat's eyes bitterer than the gorse petals. But at night it was lyrical, its double note sounded under the stars in counterpoint to the fall of the waves.

There are nights that are so still
that I can hear the small owl calling
far off, and a fox barking
miles away. It is then that I lie
in the lean hours awake, listening
to the swell born somewhere in the Atlantic
rising and falling, rising and falling
wave on wave on the long shore
by the village, that is without light
and companionless. And the thought comes
of that other being who is awake, too,
letting our prayers break on him
not like this for a few hours,
but for days, years, for eternity.

———◇———

The end of a peninsula is a long way from anywhere, but with the help of the motor they found it. All that way to eat ice-cream; to raise the newspaper as protection from the beauty of the sea. They consumed chips and beer. With bellies a-flame from the scorching of the salt sun, they lurched at night from the inn to the churchyard, knowing one another to the tombstones' rigid distaste.

You have to imagine
a waiting that is not impatient
because it is timeless. How long
from *habilis* to *erectus*,
from the gill to the lung?
The eye closed and the dinosaurs
were no more. It opened again
on Greece, London. The lids
are beginning to grow
heavy. The nictitating membrane
will come down to lift
on a planet gone under
the ice or water. What matter
for grief? The stars are as dew
in its world, punctuating
an unending story. It is the spirit-
level which, if love cannot
disturb, neither can evil.

There were other churches from which the population had withdrawn, Celtic foundations down lanes that one entered with a lifting of the spirit, because there were no posts, no telegraph wires. Is God worshipped only in cathedrals, where blood drips from regimental standards as from the crucified body of love. Is there a need for a revised liturgy, for bathetic renderings of the scriptures? The Cross always is avant-garde.

The church is small.
The walls inside
white. On the altar
a cross, with behind it
its shadow and behind
that the shadow of its shadow.

The world outside
knows nothing of this
nor cares. The two shadows
are because of the shining
of two candles: as many
the lights, so many
the shadows. So we learn
something of the nature
of God, the endlessness
of whose recessions
are brought up short by
the contemporaneity of the Cross.

—◇—

Town Christmases, country ones, sea Christmases are all transcended, perhaps, in nativities of the spirit. If one cannot have the lights and festivities of the town, one can celebrate the coming of three waves from afar, who fall down, offering their gifts to what they don't understand.

---◇---

This is the wrong Christmas
in the right place: mistletoe
water there is no kissing
under, the soused holly

of the wrack, and birds coming
to the bird-table with
no red on their breast. All
night it has snowed

foam on the splintering
beaches, but the dawn-
wind carries it away, load
after load, and look,

the sand at the year's
solstice is young flesh
in a green crib, product
of an immaculate conception.

There is a rock on the headland mentioned by Dafydd Nanmor in a *cywydd*. But it was already immemorially old in his day, five hundred years ago. The mind spun, vertigo not at the cliff's edge, but from the abyss of time. In the strong sun and the sea wind sometimes his shadow seemed more substantial than himself. But this also was part of the spilled dream.

The pound floats. The news changes
and remains the same.
There is a rock pointing
in no direction but its ability

to hold hard. Time like an insect
alights there a moment
to astonish us with its wings'
rainbow, and takes itself off.

—◇—

Because Coleridge had said that the opposite of poetry was not prose but science, that was what he preached from the pulpit at times, his eye straying through the leaded window to the sea outside that passed and remained always. He defended himself with the fact that Jesus was a poet, and would have teased the scientists as he teased Nathanael.

I have waited for him
            under the tree of science,
and he has not come;
            and no voice has said:
Behold a scientist in whom
            there is no guile.

I have put my hand in my pocket
            for a penny for the engaging
of the machinery of things and
            it was a bent
penny, fit for nothing but for placing
            on the cobbled eyeballs
of the dead.
                  And where do I go
            from here? I have looked in
through the windows of their glass
            laboratories and seen them plotting
the future, and have put a cross
            there at the bottom
of the working out of their problems to
            prove to them that they were wrong.

God's acre – not in the sea but by the sea. A place where people were buried rather than married. Compare the registers of deaths and nuptials. The earth rattled upon the coffins with the force of spray whipping across the rocks. The same melancholy hymn rose from the small groups in their cheap mourning and drifted away on the grey wind. The expensive, competitive flowers lay like flotsam cast up by the perennial tide.

Women blubbed for him
and went home. A petal blown
from time's wreath, the barn owl
came drifting. In the vicarage

hard-by on the frayed
curtains, as the lights
came on, the shadow of two
faces drew near and kissed.

—◇—

'The holiness of the heart's affections.' Never
tamper with them. In an age of science everything
is analysable but a tear. Everywhere he went,
despite his round collar and his licence, he was
there to learn rather than teach love. In the sim-
plest of homes there were those who with little
schooling and less college had come out top in that
sweet examination.

An account in paint
of the impossibility of loving
too much. A fading echo,
despite the darkness, of unquenchable
light. Character is built up
by the application of uncountable
brush strokes. Who can number
the leaves on a tree? But are people
deciduous? They burn more richly
towards old age, leisurely fountains
to which we can bring our desire
to be refreshed. I imagine an eye busy
with this, as a bee with a flower,
fertilising it while gathering nectar.

They were among Chaucer's pilgrims, but journeying towards no Canterbury. They were part of that great multitude which no man can number, but not in white clothes. They were not to be judged by him. Is there a judgment? They were part of 'life's own self-delight' from which had sprung 'the abounding, glittering jet'.

—◇—

Still going;
eighty odd years,
no grumbling.
Smoked, drank, ate

what I liked. Did
as the blood
told me. Ironed
my will on a hard

board. Complaints?
They were common:
coughs, colds, changeableness
of the heart's

weather. Took the
wet with the dry.
Chewing as much
as I bit off,

sparing the mind
its dyspepsia. Will
there be mutiny
at the day's end? The spirit

retains its poise,
ready any time now
for walking the bone's
plank over the dark waters.

Revision was in the air. Language was out of date; too formal. God was available for conversation. Bishops were overawed by the theologians. What committee ever composed a poem? Parishes were to be grouped; uneconomical churches closed. How could farm people keep abreast of the prices and help the Church make two ends meet? The lean angel picked them off by twos and threes on the way to devotion.

To the church on the hill
three women came
with the need to escape
from the echo of their silence.

One had bent bones,
one the hernia of
the spirit. One looked up
with turned eye at a half truth.

I listened to them singing
grey hymns with the mould
on them; doled them
the hard crust of communion

and the tart wine, facing them
at last with the answer
of the locked door to the question
they were too late to ask.

There are the naturals, such men 'as sleep of nights'. And there are those 'with a lean and hungry look', the hollow of cheek; the 'Hamlets pale from eating flies'. Do we know where we belong? 'Each man in his time plays many parts'. What part was he playing? Or was he just play-acting?

The piper with the thin lips
plays. I would not dance
it again, but I must, everyone
must to that insistent

music. The women of Asia
sway, the Paradise bird
advances under the rainbow
of itself; the weasel circles

the rabbit; as to a window
the fish come – all with their faces
empty, none of them conscious
of what they do. I only

look at him as I dance,
shaming him with the operation
on the intelligence of
a creature without anaesthetic.

And still it goes on. Still it went on in that parish, as in many another a parish throughout the communion. But just when, after such long practice, he was beginning to approach spiritual health, life with that irony that is so dear to it announced that there is a time to retire even from a cure.

'And what is life?'
          asked the small boy,
blowing bubbles in which
          his reflections answered:
'You must wait until you are older.'

'And what is love?'
          the young people
demanded. And the drizzling faces
          it had passed by jeered:
'You should have thought of that before.'

'Then what is truth?'
          the scholar inquired,
creeping from word to word
          in the text-book, half expecting
to come on it from behind.

'Life? Love? Truth?' the old man
          mumbled. And 'Grey-beard'
earth said in anticipation of
          its bone meal, 'you have been
up too long. It is time for bed.'

—◇—

'No man is an island.' And yet on a peninsula one is never far from the sea. There it was at his window. 'Let retirement be retirement indeed,' he exclaimed, anticipating the changes in the liturgy of the Church. But the sea revises itself over and over. When he arose in the morning or looked at it at night, it was always at a new version of it.

The pretences are done with.
The eavesdropper at the door
is a fiction. The well-bred

Amens to the formal
orisons have begun to fade.
I am left with the look

on the sky I need not
try turning into an expression.
Have I been brought here

to repent of my sermons,
to erect silence's stone over
my remains, and to learn

from the lichen's slowness
at work something of the slowness
of the illumination of the self?

From a parsonage to a cottage. The poverty of the spirit must be extended to the flesh, too; books given away, furniture dispensed with; paintings that give colour to expanses of white wall, stored away in the loft. A four-hundred-year-old cottage, that remembered centuries of Welsh tenancies. Nothing between them, too, but the unrendered slates. It was a sounding-box in which the sea's moods made themselves felt.

Here everything happens
far off. We exist
on rumours, infer
lightning from distant

reports. Is it winter
with us? It is a reflection
of unthawed clouds,
snowcaps inverted

in the Gulf Stream. We wear
sand. Owning such
wardrobe, are we uncalled-on
by the rich and famous?

From a thin sill
we look out and see even
on our worst of days
a tremendous swell coming in.

—◇—

It is always at hand; an anonymous neighbour talking always to itself; sometimes blue, sometimes grey glass, though not to be seen through. It roars and is gentle as the mood dictates. The eye is drawn to it a thousand times in a day, yet always there are the moments between, when it shows a dark fin or a white belly. And at night it is a lighted highway for the moon to my door.

The sea's surface glitters.
It is the heliograph
of the drowned, a people
reminding they are not

dead yet, prisoners rather
of that impounding water
whose walls enable
them to make light of it.

—◇—

Not from conceit certainly, yet he could not escape from his looking-glass. There it was the concealed likeness, always ahead in its ambush. Imagining the first human, he conceived his astonishment in finding himself face to face with the unknown denizen of the water. With the refinement of the mirror there occurred only the refinement of his dilemma.

The poet scans the stars
and the scientist his equations.
Life, how often must I
be brought round to confront

my image in an oblique
glass? The spirit revolves
on itself and is without
shadow, but behind

the mirror is the twin helix
where the dancing chromosomes
pass one another back
to back to a tune from the abyss.

—◇—

In need of salvation, yet not wanting to be made safe by science. The humanities are hoary. Towards the end of one's life, towards the end of the century; worse still towards the end of the millennium, the tempter approaches us as desperation.

———◇———

Fleeing for protection
from the triviality
of my thought to the thought
of its triviality – what sanctuary

there? The barbarians
are at the door. The old
forces of nihilism
and bad faith have no respect

for such altars. Dove of God,
self-powered, return
to this wrecked ark, though it be
with radiation in your bill.

The problems he had concealed from his congregations had him now all to themselves. A man who had refrained from quarrelling with his parishioners for fear of rhetoric, over what poetry could he be said to preside from his quarrel with himself?

He is his own
spy without the need
to decode the language
since he gave it us.

He is at our side,
watching the space-launch
of our prayers, their orbiting
about the wrong throne.

He listens in
at the self's councils,
planning the exercise
that will come to nothing.

He is the double agent
of life, working for
the continuance of it
by its betrayal.

He is what escapes always
the vigilance of our lenses,
the faceless negative
of himself we dare not expose.

Not without a struggle. 'Less oft is peace in Shelley's mind . . .' His belief that prayer was in silence was the un-swept room into which the seven devils of rationalistic thought would come crowding. Out of the darkness threatening to engulf him he would gasp out his entreaties against his better judgment.

—◇—

Conversation, soliloquy,
silence – a descending or an ascending
scale? That you are there
to be found, the disciplines

agree. Anonymous presence
grant that, when I come
questioning, it is not with the dictionary
in one hand, the microscope in the other.

The sea at his window was a shallow sea; a thin counterpane over a buried cantref. There were deeper fathoms to plumb, 'les délires des grandes profondeurs', in which he was under compulsion to give away whatever assurances he possessed. He was too insignificant for it to be a kind of dark night of the soul.

Hear me. The hands
pointed, the eyes
closed, the lips move
as though manipulating
soul's spittle. At bedsides,
in churches the ego
renews its claim
to attention. The air
sighs. This is
the long siege, the deafness
of space. Distant stars
are no more, but their light
nags us. At times
in the silence between
prayers, after the Amens
fade, at the world's
centre, it is as though
love stands, renouncing itself.

Yeats said he had found nothing half so good as his long sought solitude. But this one, had he ever been anything but solitary? And yet in this coastal solitude, far out on a peninsula, the breaking of which by car or aircraft he so much resented, there came to him at odd moments the wisdom of humans.

And this one writes and he knows
being wise: 'Loving
is courage; there is no fear
in love.' I take the beam
from my eye. 'Friend,'
I murmur, 'there is a mote
in yours; I will not
remove it. Here is my heart
to be hurt. Here is my hand
for blaming. I give you
myself. Scribble me
with my faults; reap
my insolvency. Am I not
also in the debt of love?'

Both female. Both luring us on, staring crystal-eyed over their unstable fathoms. After a lifetime's apprenticeship in navigating their surface, nothing to hope for but that for the love of both of them he would be forgiven.

—◇—

I look out over the timeless sea
over the head of one, calendar
to time's passing, who is now open
at the last month, her hair wintry.

Am I catalyst of her mettle that,
at my approach, her grimace of pain
turns to a smile? What it is saying is:
'Over love's depths only the surface is wrinkled.'